GRAND CANYON

BY
Jan Mell

I wish to thank Keith Miller of Grand Canyon National Park for all his help.

PUBLISHED BY

CRESTWOOD HOUSE

Mankato, MN, U.S.A.

LIBRARY OF CONGRESS CATALOGING IN PUBLICATION DATA

Mell, Jan.
  Grand Canyon

  (National parks)
  Includes index.
  SUMMARY: Describes the history, geographical features, and plant and animal life of Grand Canyon National Park. Includes a map of the park.
  1. Grand Canyon National Park (Ariz.) — Juvenile literature. [1. Grand Canyon National Park (Ariz.) 2. National parks and reserves.] I. Title. II. Series: National parks (Mankato, Minn.)
  F788.M45   1988   917.91'32 — dc19   88-18707
  ISBN 0-89686-406-5

| International Standard Book Number: 0-89686-406-5 | Library of Congress Catalog Card Number: 88-18707 |

PHOTO CREDITS

Cover: Journalism Services: Dave Brown
Journalism Services: (Dave Brown) 20, 25, 29, 30, 32, 34-35, 41
Tom Stack: (Spencer Swanger) 18; (Jeff Foott) 39
DRK Photo: (Tom Bean) 4, 6, 8-9, 11, 22, 26-27, 37; (Larry Ulrich) 12; (Pat O'Hara) 14-15; (Stephen Trimble) 17; (D. Cavagnaro) 43

Produced by Carnival Enterprises.

CRESTWOOD HOUSE

Box 3427, Mankato, MN, U.S.A. 56002

TABLE OF CONTENTS

Grand Canyon National Park.

IT REALLY IS GRAND!

There is nothing on earth like the Grand Canyon. People from all over the world come to see what nature has done. Some refer to the canyon as a "geological textbook." Each exposed layer of rock is like a page, telling something about the earth's past.

The oldest rock is at the bottom of the canyon and is in what's called the Inner Gorge. The rock here is more than two billion years old, or half as old as the earth. The sides of the canyon are made up of separate layers of rock laid down at different times in the earth's life. The youngest rock is at the top. A *geologist* can trace our planet's growth by studying the different types of rock.

The Grand Canyon is located in northwestern Arizona. From either north or south, the approach to the canyon is mostly flat. The desert land seems ordinary until you see the rim, or the edge, of the canyon. What a view! Most people are amazed at what they see. The first look seems too strange to be true. The canyon's size is too big to be believed. The Colorado River can be seen one mile down, still carving out the Inner Gorge.

The Grand Canyon is ten miles across from its North Rim to the South Rim. Each rim has its own history and unique features. To hike from rim to rim takes two days and you must walk 21 miles. The road around the

Layers and layers of rock form the spectacular Grand Canyon.

5

Grand Canyon is 214 miles.

Many artists come to the canyon rim to watch the colors change all day long. Each layer of rock has its own special color. As the sun rises and sets the canyon's colors keep changing. In the morning the colors are pastel blue, purple, and gold. At noon reds, whites, and greens fade.

When the sun moves westward, the strong colors begin to jump out. A haze begins to fill the canyon in late afternoon. By sunset the canyon is filled with a red glow. As naturalist John Burroughs said, "It's the world's most wonderful spectacle, ever changing, alive with a million moods."

Artists, photographers, and sightseers come to experience the beauty of the Grand Canyon.

PLATEAUS OF THE GRAND CANYON

The Grand Canyon is 277 miles long. The walls of the canyon drop in a series of cliffs, slopes, and terraces. The canyon walls are made up of different rock layers. Each layer *erodes,* or wears away, at a different rate. This makes the walls uneven.

The uppermost eastern part of the Grand Canyon starts at Less Ferry. It ends on the west side at the Grand Wash Cliffs, which overlook Lake Mead and the Mohave Desert.

Sixty-five million years ago the land in the Grand Canyon began to rise, creating a *plateau* (a plateau is an area of flat land that is raised above the surrounding land). The Colorado River cut through the plateau south of its center, or highest point. This made the North Rim 1,200 feet higher than the South Rim. This also made the North Rim slope toward the canyon and the South Rim slope away from the canyon. Water runs down the sides of the North Rim into the canyon. This causes more erosion on the North Rim than on the South Rim, where the water runs away from the canyon.

The land on the South Rim is called the Coconino Plateau. It is named after the Cohonia Native Americans, who lived there in 600 A.D.

The land on the North Rim is divided into four plateaus all named by the Southern Paiute Native Americans who lived there about 700 years ago.

The Kaibab (a Paiute word meaning "mountain lying down") is the plateau farthest east. It is also the highest at 7,500 to 8,500 feet above sea level. This plateau receives more rainfall than any of the other plateaus in the Grand Canyon. Therefore, it has the most plant growth. It looks like an island of trees rising from the desert.

West of the Kaibab is the Kanab Plateau (meaning "willow"). Willows lined the streambed of Kanab Creek when the Paiutes lived there.

The Kanab Plateau is separated from the Uinkaret Plateau (meaning "region of the pine") by the Toroweap Valley. This area is covered with volcanic lava flows and cinder cones.

West of the Uinkaret Plateau the land drops to the Shivwits Plateau. It is the lowest of the plateaus and the farthest west. It ends at the Grand Wash Cliffs.

FUN FACT   The cables used to build the Kaibab Suspension Bridge were too long to be taken down by mule. Instead members of the Havasupai tribe carried them on their shoulders and walked them down the South Kaibab trail. Much of the work was done at night by flood light, because the Inner Gorge was too hot during the day. It was built in 1928.

The highest plateau in the Grand Canyon is The Kaibab.

PREHISTORIC PEOPLE

The first people to look over the rim of the Grand Canyon were Native Americans. No one knows for sure when they came.

In 1933, some construction workers were building a trail in the canyon. They went exploring on their days off. In Luka Cave they found animal *figurines* made of twigs from willow and cottonwood trees. One had horns like a bighorn sheep, and another looked like a deer. A third had a twig through it, as if it had been killed by a spear. These figurines are 3,200 to 5,000 years old. They are the earliest evidence of human life around the canyon.

Since 1933, many more split-twig figurines have been found, especially in the caves in the Redwall Limestone area. Usually they are found in caves that are difficult to get to.

Historians believe that people from the Pinto-Basin Desert Culture made these twig animals. Some of them lived 8,000 years ago. They were hunters. In those days, hunting societies had rituals. They would make twig animals and pretend to kill them. By doing this, they hoped to attract real animals.

The Anasazi, also known as the Basketmakers, were the next tribe of Native Americans to live in the canyon. Their baskets, tight enough to hold water, were made of twisted yucca and other plants. They farmed corn, squash, and beans both in the canyon and on the rim. They hunted bighorn sheep, deer, and rabbit with spears and bows and arrows.

The population grew. By 1100 A.D. hundreds of people were living in the canyon. Farming had become more important, although the people still hunted and gathered food. They also planted cotton, something they learned from the Mexicans. Now they could make cloth by weaving and spinning.

The Cohonina tribe lived in the western section of the Grand Canyon at the same time the Anasazi lived in the canyon. They moved in from central Arizona. They were friendly with the Anasazi and traded with them. Like the Anasazi, they farmed and hunted. However, their houses and pottery were not as well made as the Anasazi's.

In 1150 A.D. the Anasazi and the Cohonia left the Grand Canyon. There is much debate as to why they left. Most *archaeologists* believe they left because there wasn't enough rainfall. Farming provided half their food. When they lost their crops, they had to move on.

Around 1300 the Cerbat tribe, a new people with a simpler life style,

The vastness of the Grand Canyon stretches for miles and miles.

Canoeists can travel the quiet, blue-green waters of the Little Colorado River.

moved into the Grand Canyon. They came from the West. They are ancestors of the Havasupai, the only Native Americans now living in the canyon.

The Cerbat were hunters using bows and arrows. They planted crops near permanent springs. They were very good at dressing hides, which they made into moccasins and clothing. They ate piñon nuts and agave stalks. The Hopi and the Paiute lived north of the canyon and the Cerbat traded with them.

Around the same time the Cerbat were in the canyon, the Southern Paiute came to the canyon. In summer they hunted and gathered wild plants on the North Rim. In winter they moved farther into the canyon. Here they stored seeds for winter.

The Navajo didn't come to the Grand Canyon until around 1600. They found the ruins of the Anasazi. Today their reservation covers much of northeast Arizona and extends to the edge of the Grand Canyon.

THE FIRST EXPLORERS

The first Europeans to explore the Grand Canyon were Spanish soldiers. In 1540, they were commanded by Gracía Lopez de Cardeñas and were searching for gold and riches. They met the Hopi Native Americans who showed them how to get to the South Rim. The Hopi also knew how to get down to the river, but they didn't show the Spanish soldiers. Needing water, the soldiers tried for three days to get to the river. They failed. This was not the place they had hoped it would be, and soon they left.

It is amazing that Cardeñas was able to get as far as he did. But it is even more amazing that he said very little about the Grand Canyon when he arrived home. For two centuries the Native Americans of the Grand Canyon were left alone.

In 1776, Father Franciso Tomás Garcés, a missionary with another expedition, visited the tribes near the canyon. He was interested in the people and not the Grand Canyon. He, like Cardeñas, found nothing much of interest in the Grand Canyon!

In the early 1800s, fur trading was at its peak. Trappers told everyone about Wyoming's Yellowstone and California's Yosemite areas. But they did not say much about the Grand Canyon. They knew it was there, but they considered it empty and bare. White men still couldn't reach the river and

FUN FACT Charles Dudley Warner was the first noted author to tell the world about the Grand Canyon.

Cottonwood and willow trees and many colorful birds live along the banks of Havasu Creek and Havasu Falls.

the bottom of the canyon itself. The Grand Canyon remained a mystery.

In 1858, a man by the name of Ives was the leader of another expedition. He was the first to travel up the Colorado River to Black Canyon. Here the steamboat *Explorer* was wrecked on rocks under the water near where Hoover Dam is now. Ives used a rowboat to go farther up Black Canyon. With the help of Native American guides, he and his men explored the Inner Gorge. They stayed for several days. They did not see the eastern part of the Grand Canyon at all, or even where the Colorado and Little Colorado Rivers met. As a result, the maps they later made were wrong.

Dr. John Newberry, a geologist, was the first scientist to study the Grand Canyon. He too was with the Ives expedition. Newberry knew the canyon had much to offer geologists in studying the earth's history.

In 1869, Major John Wesley Powell took a party of nine men down the Green and Colorado Rivers through the Grand Canyon. Up to this time the maps of the area were incomplete, and the Colorado River of the Grand Canyon was uncharted.

It was not an easy trip. Powell's expedition started on May 24, 1869. On June 9, one of the boats, *No-Name*, was smashed in the rapids. Two thousand pounds of supplies were lost. Fortunately the crew was saved. By July 17, food and water were in short supply. The men hunted deer and bighorn sheep for food.

On August 10, the men were in the Inner Gorge. The walls of the canyon were one mile high. There were no deer or bighorn sheep to hunt. The *rapids* were fierce, and the boats tipped and filled with water. Food was spoiled and only flour, coffee, and dried apples were left. Starving, the men raided a Native American garden of its green squash and made a squash stew. By now Powell talked of the canyon as "our granite prison."

On August 27, half-starved and water-soaked, the men came to some bad rapids. Three of the men insisted they stop, leave the boats, and hike out of the canyon to a Mormon settlement not too far away. After much thinking, Powell said no. The three men decided to leave the rest and go on alone. The last of the flour was baked into biscuits and given to all the men. Powell gave copies of his diary and notes to the three men, so if they made it out and he didn't, a record of their expedition would be saved. They also took ammunition and weapons.

Powell and his five remaining men made it through the difficult rapids to quiet water in one day's time. Unfortunately, the three men who left were

FUN FACT Zane Grey, an author of western novels, based many of his books on the Grand Canyon area.

killed by members of the Paiute tribe. The Paiute thought that the men were prospectors who had killed women of their tribe.

Powell put the Grand Canyon on the map and brought it to public attention. After a second expedition, Congress established the Geographical and Geological Survey of the Rocky Mountain Region, and made Powell its director.

With the help of an experienced rower, visitors can take a thrilling ride through the rapids of the Colorado River.

EARLY SETTLERS, TOURISTS, AND BURROS

John Hance was the first white settler in the Grand Canyon. He came in 1883 to mine asbestos, which is a mineral used in building construction. He improved an old Native American trail, but in 1884 a rockslide destroyed part of his trail. Rather then rebuild it, he started a new trail down Red Canyon. It became the New Hance Trail.

Mining was not profitable, but tourism was. In 1884, John Hance became the first tour guide and took the first family to the bottom of the canyon. Mrs. Ayer, who was one of the tourists, was the first white woman to reach the bottom of the canyon.

Hance had tourists stay in his cabin, which he called a "ranch." It was located on the South Rim. He led people on foot, horse, and mule, telling them tall tales as they went. In 1906, he moved to Bright Angel Lodge, where he was hired to greet tourists and tell them stories.

In the late 1800s, the canyon was still full of *prospectors,* people who explore for gold or other minerals. Prospecting was very difficult work. Trails had to be built. Many "trails" were only improved paths that animals and Native Americans had made. Pack animals had to carry the ore.

The *burro,* a native of North Africa, was brought into the canyon by the prospectors as a pack animal. Burros can live on almost any type of plant life, and they can move on land that is too difficult for horses and mules. Some burros escaped into the wild or were left behind by prospectors. Their numbers multiplied. They ate everything in sight, causing erosion and shortages of food for the native animals. They polluted the waters of the canyon.

By 1924, it was evident that the burros were ruining the Grand Canyon. The National Park Service killed 2,800 burros over the next 60 years. Animal lovers were outraged. By 1980, several hundred burros remained. This time the remaining burros were airlifted out of the canyon area. They were taken to Texas for adoption by private parties. Today there is a herd of 20 burros in the park, but it is a non-breeding herd.

In 1890, William Wallace Bass set up camp near Havasupai Point on the South Rim. He had come to Arizona for his health and lived on the South

A steep, narrow mule path takes visitors down to the bottom of the Canyon.

Even today, the winding Colorado River cuts deeper and deeper into the Canyon.

Rim for 40 years. He was a good friend of the Havasupai tribe and helped them establish a school. He located several copper and asbestos claims in the canyon. In Shinumo Canyon he grew melons, corn and other vegetables, grapevines, and apricot trees. He blazed new trails and led many tourists through the canyon and across the river.

In 1892, one of the people Bass guided into the Havasu Canyon was Ada Diefendorf, a music teacher. Two years later they were married. They lived at Bass Camp.

Ada became the first white woman to raise a family on the South Rim. With four children, life was not easy on the rim—Ada made a three-day trip to the Colorado River just to do the laundry!

EROSION AND FORMATION

At first glance the canyon seems too strange to be real. Huge and varied rock formations jut up in the canyon. The depth and width of the canyon seem endless. It is this vastness that is so breathtaking, making the viewer feel very tiny.

There could not have been a Grand Canyon without an uplifting of the Colorado Plateau and the cutting action of the Colorado River. The river carries large boulders and small stones. They scrape and gouge the sides of the canyon. As the river cuts downward, it exposes the canyon walls to weathering and erosion.

Some people can't believe the river could erode something as large as the Grand Canyon. They would rather believe it was an earthquake or a collapse of the earth's crust. However, the layers of rock on both sides of the canyon are identical. That means the Kaibab and Coconino Plateaus were once joined. The Colorado River must have separated them.

Weathering, the slow erosion of exposed rocks, is caused by many things: heat, cold, running water, frost, and ice. The rocks are heated in the sun, and at night the temperature drops, causing the rocks to crack. Water seeps into the cracks, freezes, and expands, causing more cracks. Light soil is formed for plants to grow. Their roots put more pressure on the rocks.

Lichen grows in small cracks. Their tiny roots cause the rocks to crack more. Lichen also makes acid that eats into the surface of the hardest rocks.

Sandstone, limestone, and *schist* are hard rocks that weather slowly and

form cliffs. *Shale* is soft and wears away to slopes. The Esplanade and the Tonto Platforms were formed when shale was eroded away, leaving platforms of harder rock.

Chemical weathering happens when moisture seeps into rocks and changes their minerals. The water dissolves some of the rock and chemically breaks down others to form clay.

Rainwater can seep into limestone and slowly hollow out caverns and underground channels. The Redwall Cliff has many caves formed in this way.

Shale becomes so weak that it can't support heavier rock above it. It slumps, and eventually there is a landslide. If shale were not in the Grand Canyon, there would be less erosion, and the gorge would be more "V" shaped.

Along with the Colorado River, streams formed by flash floods and rain storms drain the rim. Many of these have cut side canyons back into the main canyon walls.

BUILD-UP OF THE GRAND CANYON

The creation of the Grand Canyon has two parts. The first part was the build-up of the land, which took two billion years. The second part was the erosion of that same land, which took more than six million years!

Geologists are able to tell how old the rocks are in the canyon. One way they do this is by *fossil* reading. Fossils are the imprints found in rocks of plants and animals from long ago. If fossils are found in rock, we can learn how old the rock is by the types of fossils we find.

Two billion years ago the area that is now the Grand Canyon was covered with shallow water. There were active volcanoes. For millions of years, sediments from the water and lava built up in layers thousands of feet deep. More than a billion years ago, forces inside the earth caused the layers to buckle and fold and then push up. The land rose as high as the Rocky Mountains are today. The rocks were changed by tremendous heat.

The Vishnu Schist of the Inner Gorge is the oldest rock in the canyon. Red-hot material from the center of the earth was pushed up into the base of a

Throughout its 277-mile course, the Colorado River changes many times from calm water to whitewater rapids and back to calm water.

newly-formed mountain. It cooled and hardened into a pink-colored *granite*. It is now called the Zoroaster Granite, and can be seen from the Inner Gorge trail.

Most of this mountain was eroded off into a plain in the next half-billion years. The sea rose and fell many times. A second mountain range pushed up and was then worn away. Again the sea came and deposited sand to form the Tapeats Sandstone. The walls of the canyon are divided into many formations. Each formation has its own name, and each was formed by a different environment.

The rock on the top of the rim today is the Kaibab Limestone. It was laid down 230 million years ago.

To walk from the rim of the Grand Canyon to the Inner Gorge is to walk through time and color. The many layers of rock formations range in color from brown to red-orange, purple, blue-grey, and green.

THE SOUTH RIM

The South Rim is much easier to get to than the North Rim. That's why most of the visitors come here. Many visit Grand Canyon Village with its different lodges. The park headquarters is in the village, as well as two museums. The Yavapai Museum tells about the geological history of the park. The Tusayan Museum tells about the Native Americans that lived in the park long ago.

The South Rim is open all year. There is snow on this rim in the winter, but it melts quickly. Daytime temperature in the winter is in the low 40s. Night temperature is usually in the low teens and 20s. Summer temperatures range from the 80s during the day to night time temperatures in the 40s.

There are two rim trails—the South Rim nature trail and the Comanche Point trail. The Comanche is not maintained by the park. It is an old jeep road used mainly by Navajo families who live and graze sheep on reservation lands near the eastern end of the park.

The South Rim gets less rain than the North Rim. The lack of moisture makes the trees grow slowly. The main trees are the dwarfed piñon and juniper trees. Some animals found here that aren't found on the North Rim are the Abert squirrel, spotted ground squirrel, and rock pocket mouse.

FUN FACT In 1964 the American astronauts descended to the bottom of the canyon. The hike was part of their training program for their first landing on the moon!

The view of the Canyon from the South Rim is breathtaking.

Most visitors see the Grand Canyon from the South Rim, which is easier to get to than the North Rim.

THE NORTH RIM

In the early spring, members of the Anasazi tribe came up to the North Rim to live a part of each year. They left the Inner Canyon before the rocks became too hot to touch in summer. They knew that summer on the North Rim would be cool and crisp.

Hikers and backpackers also like the North Rim in summer because of its coolness. It also has a wider variety of rim trails than the South Rim.

The highest part of the North Rim is 1,200 to 1,500 feet higher than the South Rim. This height makes a lot of difference. More snow falls here because of it. Snow melts slowly, so more moisture penetrates the soil. This allows water to get down to the long roots of big fir, spruce and ponderosa pine trees.

The North Rim receives twice as much rainfall a year as the South Rim. February is the coldest month—average temperature is 9°F. In winter the North Rim can have 12 feet of snow. Because of all the snow, the North Rim is closed from the middle of October to mid-May.

The piñon pine and Utah juniper trees grow below the rim along the steep slopes of the canyon. Warm air coming up from the Inner Gorge feeds these forests. In the late summer months, the warm air from the bottom of the canyon rises. As it cools, it forms dark thunderheads. These water-filled clouds rain on the North Rim.

Away from the canyon's North Rim are forests and *meadows*. The meadows are full of spectacular wild flowers. In the spring there are acres of wild pink phlox. They grow in mats close to the ground. From a distance they look like snow.

The soil is richer here and deeper than on the South Rim. The variety of wildflowers is greater. Burrowing animals like voles, pocket gophers, and weasels live in the meadows.

Shrews, skunks, deer mice, wood rats, and horned toads make up the small animal life. Larger animals include mule deer, coyote, porcupine, some mountain lions and even a few black bear. Wild turkeys, flickers, great horned owls, and hawks live in the canyon. Large black ravens can be seen soaring over the rim. Pygmy nuthatches run headfirst down tree trunks. The Kaibab squirrel is found here in the canyon—and nowhere else in the world!

In 1906, Theodore Roosevelt decided to protect the mule deer. There was a herd of 4,000, and mountain lions were killing them. The game warden

FUN FACT The Park Service performs over 200 emergency search and rescues a year.

Fir, spruce, and ponderosa pine grow on the North Rim of the Grand Canyon.

The North Rim, which is higher than the South Rim, receives more rain and snow.

was told to kill all animals that hurt or killed the deer. Other people joined in the kill. By 1930, some 781 lions, 554 bobcats, 4,889 coyotes, and 20 wolves had been killed.

Eventually the mule deer numbered over 100,000. This was too many for the forest. The deer ate all the undergrowth. They nibbled off branches of larger trees as high as the deer could stretch. Millions of acres of wooded area became bare. The park became littered with deer that had starved to death.

In 1924, Navajo trackers were hired to move the deer from the North Rim to the South Rim, where there were fewer deer. Newspaper reporters and photographers came to record the drive. No one realized that it was impossible to move wild, half-starved deer. The deer scattered, going in all different directions. The drive was called off.

Today hunting programs outside the park help to keep the deer numbers down. But when there are mild winters, the deer population rises. Food is easier to find when there is less snow.

Deer have learned to beg for food. But feeding the deer is dangerous. They can kick, and their kick is like being hit with a hammer. Also, something could frighten the deer. It might bolt off, trampling people in its way.

INNER GORGE

Tonto Plateau is a broad bench above the Grand Canyon's Inner Gorge. It is covered with Tapeats Sandstone, which is a hard rock that is not easily eroded. In some places it hides the view of the Inner Gorge, where the Colorado River is still eroding away the hard, black rocks. These rocks are over two billion years old. They are the oldest rocks in the canyon.

A visitor can hike, take a mule trip, or boat through the Inner Gorge. It is a long hot trip, but well worth the trouble. Once in the Inner Gorge, the view upwards reveals smoky blues, pale golds, and purple shadows.

Here in the gorge, the river whooshes by. Cottonwoods and willows line Bright Angel Creek. Warblers, grosbeaks, and vireos use the leaves of the trees for cover. These trees will grow near natural springs as well as along the creek.

Vegetation is sparse because of the heat, lack of water, and poor soil. Cacti, agave, and blackbrush dot the landscape. The spotted skunk, Grand

FUN FACT In 1911, Ellsworth and Emery Kolb made the first film of the Inner Gorge and the rapids of the Colorado River. Emery built a showroom at the head of Bright Angel Trail. For 60 years he gave lectures and showed his film of the trip to tourists.

Mist from waterfalls can cool off hikers in the Inner Gorge.

Canyon rattlesnake, and chuckwalla lizard live here.

In summer, the weather is steamy. The temperature can be over 115°F. During the day, temperatures over 100°F have been recorded for every month from April through October. Shortly after sunrise the black rocks of the gorge heat up to 120°F. All day long and well into the evening, the rocks give off stored heat. Visitors who don't like heat shouldn't go into the Inner Gorge in summer.

In winter, less than an inch of snow falls in the Inner Gorge. From December through February, temperatures average 58°F during the day. Night temperatures are around 38°F.

Some of the mammals that live in the Inner Gorge come out to eat at night when it's cool. This is called a *nocturnal* way of life. The spotted skunk looks for deer mice at night. Bats search the air for insects and mule deer can be seen drinking from the river.

THE COLORADO RIVER

On September 7, 1867, James B. White was pulled from the Colorado River just below the Grand Canyon. He was half-starved and dangerously sunburned. Tied to a makeshift raft, he had floated down the Colorado River. Some people think he was the first to float the length of the Grand Canyon. He was never clear about where he entered the river. No one has ever been sure if he was the first, because of his hazy facts.

The Colorado River drops 2,200 feet in its 277-mile course through the canyon. The depth of the river ranges from 6 to 110 feet. The width of the river varies from 100 to 300 hundred feet. It has more than 150 rapids. The current in some of the rapids is so strong that it can tear off a person's clothing.

The Colorado River is one of the great rivers of America. It starts in the Rocky Mountains of Colorado and runs 1,400 miles to the Gulf of California by Mexico. The flow of water through the Grand Canyon is now controlled by Glen Canyon Dam. This dam was built in 1963 upstream from the Grand Canyon. Below the Grand Canyon is Hoover Dam, built in the 1930s.

In the 1930s and 1940s, geologists studying the western part of the canyon and lower part of the Colorado River decided the river was young. They thought it was six million years old. In 1960, geologists studying the river's upper section, or eastern part, found evidence that the river was 20 million to 30 million years old! Geologists were puzzled by this difference in age.

After much study, scientists now believe that the river in the canyon is

FUN FACT The Chuckwalla is a lizard that grows up to 18 inches long. It's often seen while hiking. When frightened, this lizard runs in between rocks. It blows itself up with air so it can't be pulled out of the rocks.

Deep in the Inner Gorge, river rafters prepare to set-up camp.

two different ages. There was an ancient river that flowed northwest, instead of southeast. It was here before the land rose and the canyon was created. With the uplift, the river began running southeast, as it does today in the western part of the canyon. This explains the difference in the age of the river.

Geologist believe that the Colorado River as we see it today formed five to six million years ago.

Early Spanish explorers called the river "Rio Colorado," which means Red River. In their time, the sand and mud in the river colored it red. Today the river seems clear, cold, and blue-green because of the Glen Canyon Dam. The dam takes much of the *sediment* out of the river.

THE HAVASUPAI TRIBE

The only Native Americans living in the canyon today are members of the Havasupai tribe. They call themselves Supai, which is also the name of their village. They live in a side canyon called Havasu Canyon. Some call it Cataract Canyon. Their name means "people of the blue-green water," which is the color of the water in Havasu Creek.

Supai Village can only be reached by foot or horseback, down the eight-mile Hualapai Canyon Trail. A helicopter also brings people in, but it's expensive and not used often.

Packhorses bring in mail and supplies. Electricity is available, but few households have telephones. There are some pre-built homes that have been helicoptered in.

Each year 20,000 people from all over the world come to see the waterfalls below the village. Each visitor to Supai Village must register at the Tourist Office and pay an entry fee. There is a campground and lodge, as well as a general store and cafe.

The Havasupai tribe numbers around 350 in the canyon. Another 50 live in other towns. They have lived in the canyon since the 12th century.

The Havasupai used to be farmers, growing corn, melons, beans, and squash. They dried and stored their produce in sealed cliff caves. In winter when supplies were low they could use their stored food. They moved to the rim and hunted deer and other wild game. They also gathered nuts.

The Havasupai were known for their excellent deer skins. They traded

Eight miles into the Canyon, Supai Village and Havasu Falls greet visitors.

36

them with the Hopi tribe for pottery. They traded with the Spanish in the 17th and 18th centuries for cattle and horses. With the coming of white people, however, their way of life changed for good. They still farm and raise cattle. During designated seasons they hunt. But tourism has become their main way of making a living.

HAVASU CREEK

Havasu Creek flows ten miles to the Colorado River. Along the way are several wonderful waterfalls. Navajo Fall, Havasu Falls, and Mooney Falls are the three main waterfalls. People swim and wade in the pools of water below these falls.

The creek is never dry. Rain in the surrounding area seeps down through the limestone and drains into the creek. As the water goes through the limestone, it picks up many minerals. These minerals settle onto the creek bottom, and make the bottom of the creek look white. The white creek bottom reflects the color of the sky. This makes the water appear to be a bright blue or blue-green. The deeper the water, the richer the color. But the water is really as clear as the water we drink.

Havasu Creek has made Havasu Canyon a beautiful oasis jumping with color. Cottonwood and willow trees line the creek. Beneath them are box elders, hackberry trees and wild grapevines.

Many colorful birds live here, including bright-red tanagers, yellow warblers, hummingbirds, and goldfinches. In and near the water are grebes, kingfishers, and great blue herons.

TASSEL-EARED SQUIRRELS AND UTAH AGAVES

The canyon is a barrier to some animals. Some live only on one side and not the other. The most famous of these animals are the two tassel-eared squirrels. One is called the Kaibab squirrel, which lives only on the North Rim. The other is the Abert squirrel, which lives on the South Rim and other places in the Southwest.

FUN FACT High on the rim overlooking the Havasupai Indian Reservation are two pillars. The Native Americans call them the Wigeleeva. They also call them God and Goddess and believe they watch over their crops. If the pillars should fall, the myth says, the village would die.

38

The Kaibab squirrel lives only on the Grand Canyon's North Rim.

At one time, it is believed, the Abert squirrel lived on the entire area. As the canyon became deeper, the climate changed and the Abert squirrel became trapped on the North Rim. As time passed, its color changed to a black belly and a white tail. It's name also changed, to Kaibab squirrel.

The Abert squirrel, on the South Rim, has stayed the color it always was—a dull grey tail with a white belly.

The two squirrels are much the same, except for color. They depend on the ponderosa pine for food and cover. They can live only where the ponderosa grows.

The most striking of wildflowers is the Utah agave. It is found from river to rim. At the end of a 15-to 20-year life, it blooms and then dies. From its center it sends up a 3-to 14-foot-high flower stalk. Two-thirds of the way up the stalk hang clusters of yellow flowers.

39

HIKING THE GRAND CANYON

There are two ways to see the Grand Canyon, from the rim or hiking into the canyon itself. Most visitors see the canyon only from the rim. But more than 30,000 people hike into the canyon every year. The park limits the number of backpackers in the canyon to protect the park from overuse.

Canyon hiking is the opposite of mountain hiking. The beginning of the trip is downhill. The most endurance is needed at the end of the trip for the steep climb out. A good rule to remember: it takes twice as long to hike out of the canyon as it takes to hike in.

The Grand Canyon is a desert, and water is hard to find. It's important to carry enough water and to keep drinking it, otherwise *dehydration* may become a problem. It is best not to hike into the canyon in summer, when the temperature in the Inner Gorge can be 120°F.

Stay on the trail, whenever possible. If you must leave the trail, walk on rocks, not plants. Desert vegetation can take hundreds of years to recover, if at all.

The Grand Canyon has 38 hiking trails that cover 400 miles. The three main trails from rim to river are Bright Angel and South Kaibab on the South Rim and the North Kaibab. They are referred to as the Cross-Canyon Corridor. Once on the bottom of the canyon, hikers cross the river on the Silver Suspension Bridge or the Kaibab Suspension Bridge.

Other rim-to-river trails that are also used, but they are not maintained by the park. Seven start from the South Rim and three begin from the North Rim. These trails are for experienced hikers.

VISITING THE GRAND CANYON

There are information centers on both rims. Park rangers are available to help visitors. When entering the park, visitors are given a pamphlet that tells all about the activities of the park and its facilities. There are many things to do. Here are a few ideas:

Take a mule trip down the canyon and back up or stay overnight at

Wildflowers add color to the hot and dry Inner Gorge.

Phantom Ranch and ride back up the next day.

Hike the many trails either on the North or South Rim or to the bottom of the canyon.

Stay overnight in a campground or at Phantom Ranch at the bottom of the canyon. Or stay overnight at a campground on one of the rims.

Fish in the Colorado River. Take a boat or raft trip down the Colorado River.

Stand at one of the look-out points on the North or South Rim and view the canyon through a coin-operated telescope.

Take a guided nature walk on one of the trails on either the North or South Rim.

Sleep and eat for a few days in the only lodge on the North Rim or one of the many lodges on the South Rim.

Ride in a bus and have a guide show and tell you all about the canyon.

TAKING CARE

The Grand Canyon is steep and rugged. Water is scarce all year. Heat inside the canyon is extreme in summer. In winter the trails on the rim and partially down the canyon can be full of snow and ice. The temperature can be below freezing.

Hikers must be aware of the dangers in hiking the Grand Canyon. And they must be aware of their own abilities. The first-time hikers of the canyon should stay on maintained trails and protect themselves against health hazards.

Dehydration happens with the loss of body fluids. It kills more people in the Grand Canyon than any other cause. By the time a hiker feels thirsty, he already is becoming dehydrated. Hikers, to avoid dehydration, must drink all the time, even when they don't feel thirsty.

Heat stress happens along with dehydration, and involves loss of essential body salts. A person suffering from heat stress has a headache, then begins to feel nauseated, and is sweating excessively. If anyone stops sweating and the pulse becomes rapid, get medical help. It has become a life-threatening situation.

Hypothermia is the loss of body heat from exposure to cold, wet, and windy weather. It happens mostly when the temperature is below 50°F. To prevent hypothermia, dress warmly.

Poisonous animals in the Grand Canyon are rattlesnakes, scorpions, Gila monsters, and some spiders. Most hikers are not bothered by these animals, since they only bite if frightened. But it's a good idea to wear boots and long pants for protection. Often these animals live under rocks and in bushes. Scorpions are nocturnal, which means they feed at night. Therefore, use flashlights when walking in the dark. Shake out boots and clothes before putting them on. Don't unroll sleeping bags until they are going to be used.

Cactus spines are another danger. They are not poisonous, but they can cause pain. It's best not to touch them.

By following the park's rules and being careful, a visit to Grand Canyon National Park can be fun and exciting!

By following the many hiking trails, backpackers can experience the full beauty of the Grand Canyon.

FOR MORE PARK INFORMATION

For more information about Grand Canyon National Park, write to:

Grand Canyon National Park
Box 129
Grand Canyon, AZ 86023

Havasa Canyon
Havasupai Tourist Enterprise
Supai, AZ 86435

PARK MAP

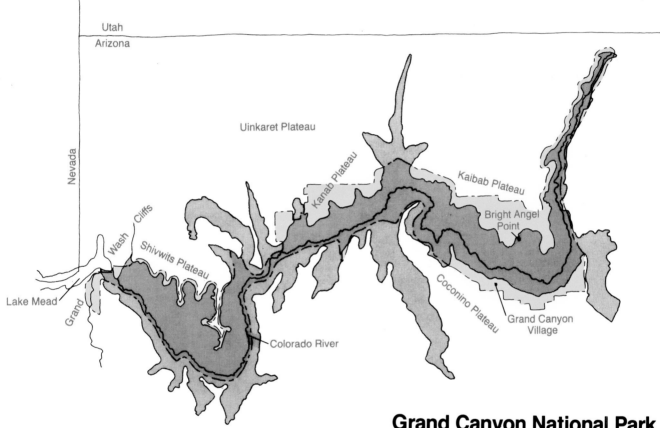

Utah
Arizona

Nevada

Uinkaret Plateau

Kanab Plateau

Kaibab Plateau

Bright Angel
Point

Wash Cliffs

Shivwits Plateau

Coconino Plateau

Lake Mead

Grand

Grand Canyon
Village

Colorado River

Grand Canyon National Park

GLOSSARY/INDEX

WEATHERING *21* — Physical or chemical changes to the earth. Physical weathering happens when the elements — heat, cold, running water, frost and ice — break rocks into pieces. Chemical weathering happens when water seeping into rocks chemically changes their minerals, to form clay.